i

Mental Toughness
Unleash the Power Within

Mental Toughness
Unleash the Power Within

How to Develop the Mindset of a
Warrior, Defy the Odds, and Become
Unstoppable at Everything You Do

Kyle Faber

Mental Toughness – Unleash the Power Within

How to Develop the Mindset of a Warrior, Defy the Odds, and Become Unstoppable at Everything You Do

Published by CAC Publishing LLC

ISBN 978-1-950010-19-6 paperback

ISBN 978-1-950010-18-9 eBook

We all have a warrior inside of us waiting to be unleashed. Once we learn how to release it we become unstoppable forces of nature that can accomplish the impossible. It's time to let your warrior out and take control of your destiny.

This book is dedicated to the warriors who have yet to be discovered.

Contents

Introduction

Although the phrase "mental toughness" has long been used informally, the term has really come into its own in the fields of sports, coaching, and business leadership, and has moved into the health, occupational, social, and educational spheres. There are even attempts being made to come up with a formal definition for "mental toughness" as a psychological construct.

During the past decade, increased attention has been paid to the qualities of mental toughness and grit. In particular, ground-breaking work by University of Pennsylvania researcher Angela Duckworth shone the spotlight on what she termed "grit" as being a defining quality in success and achievement. As it turns out, "grit" or "mental toughness" are more responsible for success in any field of endeavor and in life than intelligence, natural talent, or leadership potential.

In actuality, the idea that "mental toughness" is necessary for success is not new. The ancient Romans believed that the mind was the cradle of fortune – not just any mind, but a well-formed mind that could withstand the rigors of the path to success. Julius Cesar epitomized what it meant to have a tough mind. He could battle alongside his men without trepidation, all the while plotting strategies for individual combat and the overall battle. Similarly, it was commonly said that there was no weapon in all of Greece more lethal than the mind of Alexander the Great.

So, just what is "mental toughness"?

"I know it when I see it." That was what United States Supreme Court Justice Potter Stewart famously said in 1964 to explain how he decided whether material he was considering was obscene or not. In the same way, most people know "mental toughness" when they see it.

Mental toughness is often misunderstood. It isn't about having a strong will or a stubborn nature. Also, it is usually thought of as something you are born with or not, but, due to the brain's neuroplasticity, anyone who wants to can increase their own mental toughness.

This book takes a broad approach to the concept. Mental toughness is the product of many identifiable separate elements that you can practice individually, and then put together to reap the benefits of a tougher, more resilient mind. This book is laid out to consider each element on its own merits. You can identify each element within yourself and look for the ways that are best for you to cultivate it. Helpful exercises and strategies are sprinkled throughout the book.

You'll need to decide for yourself what "mental toughness" means to you and what you consider its defining traits and qualities. However, no matter which characteristics you choose to emphasize in your own personal version of "mental toughness," there are a couple of things to remember. First, maintaining consistency in the traits matters. Second, while "mental toughness" is an abstract concept, it is tied to actions in the real world. No matter which of the traits you focus on, the way that mental toughness is expressed is through how you act and live.

Finally, all roads in "mental toughness" lead back to "perspective." So, this book begins with "perspective." It is the frame of reference through which you view your life and every experience and event that comprises it. If your perspective is skewed, then all that comes from it will be skewed, including "mental toughness."

Perspective leads directly into the topic of "detachment," which is a very special kind of perspective. The ability to detach yourself from what is going on around you is a key component of mental toughness and contributes to emotional stability.

From there, we look at change, readiness to face challenges, and strength. Self-awareness and self-validation are also part of mental toughness. Those qualities, plus focus, a positive outlook, patience, and endurance, all contribute to self-control, a hallmark of mental toughness. And finally, we wrap up our examination of the qualities that go into mental toughness with acceptance.

No matter how you define "mental toughness" for yourself, whichever attributes you think most contribute to it, if you make the effort to improve your own mental toughness, you will be rewarded. You will experience an increased ability to handle pressure, adversity, obstacles, challenges, and failure, stronger confidence, self-belief, and motivation, and greater resilience and perseverance. Becoming more mentally tough will improve your life and experience in every area.

Chapter 1: Perspective

According to Viktor Frankl, survivor of Auschwitz and an example of extreme mental toughness, the one thing that cannot "be taken from a man" is "the last of the human freedoms – to choose one's attitude in any given set of circumstances, to choose one's own way." Frankl is talking about our freedom to choose our perspective, how we see things.

Perspective can be variously described as attitude, viewpoint, point-of-view, frame of reference, or even as "slant" or "angle" on things. Ultimately, perspective is the "lens" through which we "see" everything, be it physical or non-physical, both in the world around us and in the world within us. Fortunately, we can choose our own perspective – and it is both our ultimate freedom and the core of mental toughness.

We tend to talk about perspective using visual metaphors and analogies because those are the easiest ways to understand it. One way to think of our mental perspective is as being like a camera lens. That lens intervenes to frame and shape what we "see." There are close-up, wide-angle, aerial, and any number of other types of shots that can be taken of the same scene. There are slow shots and high-speed ones. There are all sorts of filters that can be introduced to change the image, as it is taken, from what it originally looks like, that color it or distort it, that highlight one aspect over another. Then, after the image is taken, there are an unlimited number of things that can be done to change it even more, until it no longer resembles the original at all. Our individual perspectives are just like that.

Our perspective shapes not only what we perceive (or don't) through all our senses, but also everything that we think. Conversely, what we perceive and think influences our perspective. In other words, there is a constant interplay, back and forth, between perspective and perception/thought, each influencing the other in a dynamic dance that takes on a life of its own.

We begin this book with perspective because it underpins almost everything having to do with mental toughness. Scratch the surface of any quality that contributes to mental toughness, and you are going to find "perspective" at the heart of it.

So, what are those perspectives? Where do they come from? How do they influence us? And, more importantly, do we have any control over them?

To take control of our own perspectives, we need to understand their role in perception and cognition. Our minds use perspective to process new inputs and thoughts, to organize and interpret them, placing those new inputs and thoughts in the context of existing mental constructs. In turn, the mind also uses those new inputs and thoughts to change or revise our existing perspectives, which, in turn, also alters pre-existing perceptions (i.e. memories). This capacity to change perspectives makes the human mind a very dynamic and powerful tool – which can work in your favor or against you.

We can consider perspective from two different directions. First, there is the way our brain processes our perceptions, that is, perspective as it interplays with our physical interactions with the world. The second approach to perspective has to do with the way we think and understand anything, the cognitive aspects of perspective.

Starting from sensory perceptions, and using a familiar contemporary analogy, we could say that there is a "virtual reality" platform in our head, and that what we react to is that virtual reality, not to what is "out there" in the physical world outside the body. Without this virtual reality platform in our head, it wouldn't be possible to use the input from the "real world" and the feedback from our senses intelligently.

To be able to navigate and function in the world around us, there is a chasm we need to bridge between that world and what goes on with the neurons between our ears. We preplan our activities in the physical world in our virtual world, and, if everything is consistent, then we feel safe and confident in our decisions and actions, coherent in our understanding of the world.

For the events in our internal virtual world and our external physical world to match up, we create simulations of the objects and experiences of the physical world within our virtual world. When our senses detect an object in the real world, and also find it in our mental virtual world, then we receive signals of familiarity, and other signals such as comfort – or discomfort.

Have you ever been in a new place, and felt an "unreal" sensation or a sense of heightened awareness? Those sensations are triggered when your virtual world isn't congruent with your external environment, and your mind is attempting to absorb the new data to create a mirror of it in that virtual environment. Someone who is highly sensitive to those sorts of changes can feel immense discomfort when their virtual world differs from the real world.

That virtual platform allows us to foresee the consequences of known actions. If we see an object that looks like a glass jar in the real world, or even in our imagination, then a simulation can be run in the virtual world in our head that results in the jar shattering if it were to fall to the ground. That virtual event tells us to be careful around that object in the real world – if we don't want it to break.

Without a framework through which we can understand things, we would experience chaos, instability, and failure. Without a consistent basis for understanding the world, we wouldn't be able to decide on a path and follow it. We really wouldn't be able to do much of anything.

The perspective created by our virtual mental world creates expectations. Those expectations can be disappointed or satisfied by our experiences in the real world. The differences between our perspectives or mental frameworks and our actual experiences can be felt as exciting novelty or as jarring and disturbing cognitive dissonance. Ultimately, we need to strike a balance between anchoring ourselves to what we know and liberating ourselves to experience what we don't know.

So far, we've mostly been talking about perspective in the limited sense of a degree of matching between a "virtual reality" in the mind and the "real world" experienced through the senses. That's one sort of perspective, and it's crucial for life.

Theoretically, we could say that we have been talking about a "truth" not colored by perspective, about a consistency of our perception of objects with the objects as they are. A round orb is a round orb, is a round orb. But, no matter how close the match may be, our perceptions are always mediated by perspective, and it doesn't take much to get to the real significance of perspective. To a boy in Catalonia, that round orb may be a soccer ball, a snow globe to a little girl in Vladivostok, a planet to an astronomer in California, or a cannon ball to a history buff. A simple shape can have a thousand different meanings according to the perspective of the person. Abstract art embodies this principle, being less about the image than it is about the viewer. "Beauty lies in the eye of the beholder" is the quintessential statement about perspective.

The farther you move out from the most elementary sensory experiences of concrete physical objects, the more significant perspective is. Even at the most basic level, interpretation and meaning immediately start to come into play. That round orb could be a specific berry. To a species of bird able to digest that berry, it could mean "food" and "survival." To a human being, that round orb could mean "poison" or "death" – or "power" if deliberately fed to murder the leader of a group. Moving outward, each of those meanings are then filtered through yet other layer of perspective. One may regard the murder of the leader as a cruel and greedy wrong, while another perspective may see it as the rightful end for a despot who has inflicted a nightmare upon others.

Let's put it another way. If you were watching that murder of the leader on TV, how you react to it will depend on whether you realize that you are watching a fictional detective movie, or the evening news. How you react to exactly the same perceived image depends on your perspective on the matter.

As we can see, perspective can change how we understand almost anything, even a simple round orb, even turning it into its opposite. The perspectives you hold, often without realizing it, can range from the simple and inconsequential to the complex and life-changing (even when murder isn't involved).

Consider the case of the zippered sweatshirt known as the "hoodie." Several controversies have erupted in the news over the wearing of a hoodie, because some associate the garment with a specific kind of person or situation. Your perspective will influence how you see a person wearing a hoodie, depending on which side of the controversy you land on. That's a kind of perspective that might be considered a bias.

Other kinds of biases are harder to recognize, and, if necessary, change or overcome. You aren't likely to detect them unless you are intentionally looking for them. These unconscious perspectives (biases) influence the way you think and act, even how you feel, because they are what you have always known, your unexamined "truths." They are part of the systemic framework for the way you understand yourself, others, the world, and your place in it. Generally, you only notice those unconscious perspectives when you pause to step back for a different view, when someone asks you to look differently at it, or when you experience a powerful clash with other perspectives.

In our world, we are constantly confronted by the push-pull of these kinds of frameworks, and the conflicts between those who want to maintain them and those who want to expose and change them. For example, for centuries, women and men have been attempting to untangle the subtle (and not so subtle) biases that privilege the positions of men in society, even in the minutia of daily life. These kinds of biases are perspectives that have become built into language, social structures, and known "facts," and they influence our judgements and perceptions. They are the mental frameworks that are learned from the earliest days of a person's life.

For example, these frameworks can influence the way we usually interpret the volume and force of someone speaking, based on whether the speaker is a man or a woman, boy or girl. The same sentence spoken at exactly the same volume and pace can be interpreted in completely different ways according to those internalized frameworks. We may take that interpretation (i.e. the result of perspective) as "fact" – without our ever realizing it.

Everywhere you look, there are different perspectives – between cultures, social groups, ideologies, individuals, and even within a single individual at different times or in different circumstances. Each individual has their own unique combination of perspectives through which they filter their experiences and thoughts. These perspectives develop through what they are taught, explicitly and implicitly, through experiences, and through what they choose to think.

Although the human experience exposes us to situations and trainings that can instill deeply held biases and perspectives through which we filter everything, the brain is malleable. You can change even those perspectives you have practiced your entire life. As Socrates has been famously credited with saying, "The unexamined life is not worth living." Examining even your most dearly held perspectives can add immeasurable value to your life.

You aren't stuck with a perspective that isn't serving you. Perspectives are changeable. Just as you can change a camera lens or adjust a camera setting to alter what you "see," you can alter your own perspective to one that is more useful, to one that provides you with greater mental strength and resilience.

Your first step to increasing your mental toughness is having the simple but all-important recognition that perspective shapes your perceptions and even what you accept as "facts." The second step is realizing that your perspectives are not carved in stone, they are malleable. You can change your perspective – and therefore how you perceive things, what you think, and how you feel. You have the freedom to choose your own perspective.

The single most important thing you can do on a regular basis arises out of those two recognitions: question assumptions. The more automatic your interpretation, the more "knee-jerk" your assumption about something is, the more valuable it is to question it, to ask whether you really "know" that, or if something different or more might be going on than what you can see from your current perspective.

In the next chapter, we look at "detachment," which is a very special type of perspective, one pivotal to your ability to change your other perspectives when you want to. It is also the single most important type of perspective to work on developing in the pursuit of mental toughness.

Chapter 2: Detachment

Detachment is a very special kind of perspective. Without a doubt, it is the single most important and powerful type of perspective you can learn to practice. Detachment, at its simplest, means pulling oneself back from immersion in the in-the-moment experience to "see" it from a broader perspective and context.

Detachment is really a kind of meta-perspective, a perspective that allows you to perceive (and change) the other perspectives you might have. It also allows a respite from the turmoil a perspective fully immersed in immediate experience can generate.

Countless philosophies, religions, and spiritual traditions have taught the practice of detachment as the answer to the human condition of suffering. Life is full of setbacks and sorrows. We know that. We all experience our own share. Detachment provides a perspective from which we can view those sufferings with greater equanimity, giving us greater mental strength and resilience.

The opposite of detachment is "attachment." Traditions such as Buddhism teach non-attachment as a way to achieve peace and enlightenment. Being attached to the things of this world, to emotions and desires, to judgments, to outcomes, and even attachment to your own thoughts, can trap you on a continuous roller-coaster of desire, fear, and anger. Being excessively attached to anything can result in having distorted perspectives that are the opposite of the healthy perspectives that contribute to mental toughness.

An important distinction must be made here though. The kinds of detachment and non-attachment that contribute to mental toughness are not the extreme forms of detachment, disassociation, and inability to attach that are considered serious psychological disorders and impairments.

Healthy forms of detachment and non-attachment do not exclude the human experiences of attachment to others or of being fully present in emotional and sensory experiences, or even being passionate. Rather, the kinds of detachment and non-attachment that contribute to mental toughness are volitional practices that allow a person to achieve optimal personal potential.

There are two types of detachment that really contribute to mental toughness. One is a regular practice of adopting a detached perspective. The other is detachment as an immediate response to whatever is going on in the moment. That momentary detachment can be used as an antidote to the natural tendency to become swept up in reactions to what is going on in the now.

Temporary detachment is a powerful strategy for everyone dealing with emotions in the moment, especially when those emotions are overwhelming. It is even more than valuable for empaths or those who struggle with emotional disorders like anxiety or Borderline Personality Disorder. Extreme or overwhelming emotions, whether picked up from surroundings or experienced in reaction to surroundings, can be debilitating. Detachment is the best way to stop that in its tracks, while you catch your breath, and do a "reset."

Practicing temporary detachment starts with mentally deciding that you don't need to absorb everything or react to everything all the time. Realize that you do have the power to extricate yourself from your current perspective and rise above it in one way or another. The next chapter, on emotional stability, includes a proven technique for having a valuable moment of detachment to counteract overwhelming emotions and reactions.

A lot of the time, however, all it takes to achieve immediate detachment is physically remove yourself from a situation. Have you ever been in a club that was just too loud? Have you ever been disturbed by an acquaintance telling tales about others? Or maybe you have been frustrated by a roommate with no boundaries. Sometimes, the best way to handle a situation is just to withdraw from it – go for a walk, have a cup of coffee, go to a friend's place.

Breathing and walking away is a simple fix. Walking works well, in and of itself. It increases your oxygen intake, it creates a rhythm with each step you take, and it burns off excess fight-or-flight neurotransmitters and stress hormones. As you walk away to clear your head, most things tend to right themselves at that point. When you aren't in the middle of the chaos, you aren't complicating the situation with your reactions.

The second kind of detachment requires a more substantial change in mental perspective. Establishing a perspective of detachment can be an on-going endeavor that may even become your new normal if you choose to invest the effort.

Detachment, as a perspective, is not the same as not caring, and it doesn't mean being obtuse or oblivious to reality. You can be detached while still being fully aware of the situation at hand, and you should be. Sometimes that's easier said than done, but detachment without knowing what is really going on is denial, at best, and blindness, at worst. Detachment isn't about burying your head in the sand.

A detached perspective is about remaining "present" but also "seeing" the experience from a broader viewpoint, without being attached to it or its outcome, and without being swept up by your emotional responses. There is a positive correlation between the level of detachment you are able to practice in an area and the amount of success you are able to achieve in it. Being able to adopt a detached perspective is a vital skill for success.

So, just what are you detaching from when you adopt a detached perspective?

One of the most common and powerful forms of detachment you can foster in yourself is detachment from outcomes. Not being attached to the outcome of what you are doing, whether good or bad, success or failure, allows you to be fully involved in the moment. It also helps you get back up and keep going after failures or disappointment. When you have developed mental toughness, you are able to "put things into perspective" and realize that the path to success is through the land of repeated failure.

A well-known example illustrates this. When Thomas Edison was working to develop the light bulb, power generation systems, and the electrical grid, he experienced a tremendous number of failures along the way, certainly more than 1,000, but he pressed on. Clearly, he had tenacity, but, more importantly, Edison was able to detach himself from the outcomes of his experiments, whether they were successes or failures, and hold the perspective that failures were necessary to learning. Instead of attaching any stigma to failure, Edison embraced failure, turning it to his advantage by seeing it as a necessary part of success.

Stepping back and observing your own thoughts with detachment is also powerful. Instead of experiencing your own thoughts as "precious," you can realize that your thoughts are not "reality," and are therefore not as important as they sometimes feel. You can witness the passing parade of thoughts without being attached to or disturbed by them, and you can recognize that not all thoughts need to be acted on or given undue attention.

Adopting a practice of daily reflection, especially written reflection, provides an opportunity to review your experiences, your thoughts, and who you are from a perspective of greater detachment. It not only builds the skill of detachment, it also aids in the discovery of new, more useful perspectives that contribute to mental toughness. Reflection is the act of deliberately giving deep consideration to something you might not otherwise have given much thought to.

Reflection allows you to make sense of something in a new way, by stepping back to explore other perspectives on it. When you first face a situation, you don't see all of its facets, and you naturally react to what you do see. But the bigger truth isn't always what's obvious, and jumping to a immediate reaction may just exacerbate the problem.

When you reflect, you should revisit the salient points of your day, including things that have disturbed you, and aroused fear, disappointment, or unhappiness. Consider those things, dissecting them to uncover the hidden wisdom in the mistakes, mishaps, and misfortunes. If you take the view that there is a reason for everything, and everything has consequences, even if it isn't apparent at the time, you can discover it on reflection, and that will give you more power over the event the next time it happens.

Conversely, cultivating a stance of detachment makes it easier to reflect on what happens to you and gain insight from it – and can give you the wisdom to know that most things that happen are not existential threats, so that you are better able to handle it. When you know a moment cannot affect you, it gives you the kind of strength that is easy to recognize as a form of mental toughness.

Finally, detachment, as it applies to mental toughness, is a state of acceptance and assurance that crisis or chaos doesn't have to have a lasting impact on your life if you remain detached. On the other hand, if you dive head-first, immersing yourself in bad situations, tackling them without the benefit of rational and reasoned thought, then

the chaos not only becomes real, it can spread
into the other areas of your life.

Chapter 3: Emotional Stability

The ability to practice detachment and control your own perspective is the primary basis for the emotional stability required as a foundation for mental toughness.

When you say something like, "I woke up on the wrong side of the bed today," you are really talking about a "state" you have found yourself in. You have no explicit reason to be upset or moody, but you are. We've all been there.

Our "state" – if we are in a "good state," a "bad state," or something in between – will influence our perspective, if we let it. But we can also tackle it from the opposite direction and use perspective to change our state. Adopt a powerful, strong-minded perspective, and you feel like a champion. Adopt a negative or defeatist perspective, you can feel broken.

Emotional stability is brought about by approaching it from several directions. The first is to understand the ebb and flow of emotions without becoming too caught up in it. Is the state you are in, at the moment, a good feeling or a bad feeling? If it feels good, ride the wave. If it feels bad, either do something about it or ride it out.

Emotional stability comes with recognizing that emotions are transitory and temporary states. Wait a little while and a different emotional state will soon come around. Sometimes there is nothing to be done. Sometimes it is simply better not to become caught up and immersed in what is a passing wave. Practicing detachment and releasing any attachment to the emotional wave allows it to ebb and flow.

Part of emotional stability is the ability not to be unduly swayed by external emotional triggers or events. Advertisements that seek donations, for instance, pull at your heartstrings by beginning with a sad story. They want you to have an emotional reaction so that you will give to their cause. Manufacturers determine production outputs and ramp up resource allocation according to Consumer Confidence metrics, because it is such a powerful emotional predictor of consumer behavior. In other words, when people feel good, they tend to buy things.

People who are mentally tough manage their emotions and decide whether or not to be influenced by emotional considerations, as they move toward the objective they have set their sights on. Being swept up, willy-nilly, by whatever emotions, thoughts, and reactions to events that come along isn't mental toughness. When it gets out of hand, it can even enter the realm of neurotic weakness. Any strategy that helps you think through a situation before your emotions are affected by it can help you become more emotionally stable.

Practicing detachment is one way to use perspective to achieve emotional stability. Detachment allows you to put some distance, even a barrier, between you and your perceptions and thoughts so that they don't automatically trigger your sensitivities. This is especially important if you are very empathic and connect strongly to events and people around you. Being able to control how you react to events is the biggest part of being emotionally stable.

Another way to use perspective to achieve greater emotional stability is to realize that, in any moment, the perspective you take to anything is a choice. You can choose how you "see" something. You can use your perspective to maintain emotional stability in virtually any situation. If you choose to see something as "good," then you can experience it as good, but if you choose to see something as "negative," you will experience it negatively. If you can change your perspective, which alters what you "see" and experience, then you can create an emotionally stable state for yourself.

Another shift of perspective can be a powerful catalyst for achieving emotional stability, and that is finding forgiveness. You need to forgive what offends and upsets you, not just people who

1) Detachment is needed so you do not take everything personally

Detachment is needed so you don't seek their validation that it changes your own opinion.

Detachment is needed to understand love is about acceptance not control.

36

offend you but also things that vex you, events that don't live up to expectations, disappointments, and frustrations. Forgive all of it – and when you do, you will start to build a kind of shield that is impenetrable to the troubles and aches you encounter.

Viktor Frankl, author of *Man's Search for Meaning*, wrote, "Between stimulus and response there is a space. In that space is our power to choose our response. In our response lies our growth and our freedom."

Emotional stability begins in the silence of solitude. If you can create a pause where you can process something before reacting to it, you prepare yourself, even choosing the best perspective to take, and you can become more centered and stable.

The mind cannot process anything when it is in an unstable state of chaos, drowning in the depths of frustration, or wallowing in the quicksand of misery. It's not easy to remember this while you are in the middle of a crisis. It is exactly when emotional stability and mental toughness is needed the most but is the most elusive.

To counteract the mind's natural tendency to get caught up in reactions, you can train your mind to pause every time before reacting. Catastrophes are not always born out of actions, but often out of reactions – especially ones made in haste. The more urgent the matter, the more hasty the reaction, the less considered the decisions made. A momentary pause before reacting is a moment of detachment, a moment devoted to gaining a more stable, useful, and powerful perspective.

Many types of therapy, including CBT (Cognitive Behavioral Therapy) and DBT (Dialectical Behavioral Therapy), teach the **STOPP** technique for creating that momentary pause between stimulus and response. When faced with a situation that is triggering a reaction, simply take the following steps:

1. **S**top,
2. **T**ake a breath,
3. **O**bserve,
4. **P**ull back to get perspective, and
5. **P**ractice and proceed with what works.

Training yourself into the habit of taking a simple momentary pause between the trigger and your reaction to it makes all the difference in the world – especially if you are prone to emotional reactivity. But this technique can also provide stability at any time, as life offers up a veritable roller-coaster ride of opportunities to react.

It is a very deep instinct to react instantaneously with a fight/flight/freeze reaction when an internal alarm is triggered, a primitive instinct that allowed our species to flourish. Whether you stay to "fight," turn to "flee," or simply "freeze," your response to a perceived emergency changes your physiology and mental state. That natural instinctual reaction can either contribute to or hinder mental toughness, depending on the circumstances.

We still need that fight/flight/freeze instinct, on occasion. If you were cornered in a dark alley, you'd want to react instantly to the danger, but that instinct also pops up unwarranted and unwanted, in ways that weaken our ability to function most effectively. As humans, we have evolved our civilizations and external technologies at a rate that has outpaced our genetic ability to adapt our physiological reactions to danger. So, instead of relying on raw instinct, we need to mitigate those inner uprisings with our mind – through the discipline of pausing before reacting, and with reasoning.

Reasoning allows you to analyze the situation facing you. Instead of running away, or creating an untenable situation with bravado, or freezing like a deer in the headlights, reasoning can open up other options. Our mind gives us other choices, if only we take a moment to think rather than being overwhelmed by the adrenaline of the fight/flight/freeze response coursing through our system. This takes practice, but it is an important component of mental toughness. You need to practice this before you find yourself in the situation. You can create a habit of stopping fear in its tracks by pausing for a moment of detachment that allows you to think before the reaction gets out of hand.

Emotional stability is really about being able to control the intensity of your emotions so that they remain discernable but aren't distracting or overwhelming. That provides you with all the richness and value of a full emotional life, while providing you with the emotional stability that is a key component of mental toughness.

Chapter 4: Willingness to Change

Emotional stability doesn't mean staying the same all the time or stubbornly holding to a position, and it doesn't imply being unwilling or unable to change. Change and stability are not in conflict. In fact, they are inextricably intertwined. Emotional stability makes it easier to change when desired or needed. Being flexible and willing to change are as necessary to genuine mental toughness as being emotionally stable is. Flexibility, willingness to change, and emotional stability are all rooted in perspective, especially detachment.

Conscious change doesn't come automatically. The laws of physics say that a body in motion stays in motion, and a body at rest stays at rest. That phenomenon is universal. It applies as much to human habits as it does to physical bodies in space. Nevertheless, change is a constant that touches every living and inanimate object simply because we are all the subjects of the same unrelenting ruler – time.

Mental toughness is sometimes misunderstood as stubbornness, that is, a resistance to change. Many people who try to be mentally tough just wind up being stubborn instead, by simply digging in their heels and refusing to budge. But stubbornness is more like a counterfeit version of mental toughness – it might seem to work sometimes, but stubbornness carries within itself its own weakness.

Stubbornness brings with it rigidity, while mental toughness requires flexibility and adaptability. The notion of mental toughness as a mind made of steel, unyielding, unbending, unwavering, and rejecting all kinds of onslaughts couldn't be farther from the truth. Mental toughness isn't about rigidity, it's about flexibility and adaptability – the ability and willingness to change.

Earlier, the analogy of a virtual reality platform was used to describe the way your mind interacts with your environment. That is a system of feedback that allows you to adjust, adapt, and alter your behavior as needed according to changes in your environment. Being open to feedback and being open to change based on that feedback is not only a desirable quality for mental toughness, it is also a necessary condition for life at all levels.

Do you know why the dinosaurs disappeared? They couldn't adapt to changing conditions. They were inflexible – and they aren't around anymore. That's what rigidity and the inability to change gets you. Being a "dinosaur" won't make you "mentally tough."

Instead, everywhere, the evidence is that strength and resilience comes from flexibility, not rigidity. The flexible willow branch will bend and survive the fiercest storm, while the rigid branch of a dry tree will snap off in the first bad wind. Tai Chi teaches that iron strength comes from being soft like a cloud. Tall buildings and big bridges get their strength and endurance to withstand high winds and other forces of nature from being constructed with built-in flex instead of rigid joints. That flexibility keeps them from coming apart at the seams the first time the structure is tested by the environment. During take-off, the wings of a fully loaded jet will flex upward as powerful forces press against them. The wings flex, but they don't break. If they were rigid, they'd break.

Human minds that are rigid, too, have a tendency to break, when they are tested against the forces that life brings to bear. In an even more fundamental way, at the neuronal level, the real strength and power of the human brain comes from its plasticity, from its ability to literally change its connections, rather than from hard-wiring. The ability to change is the key to successful survival at both the personal and species level.

Years ago, we witnessed a mother, obviously at wit's end, screaming at a child hypnotized by a toy store's decorations. He wouldn't budge, and his

43

mother wouldn't yield. It wasn't hard to see where the boy got his stubborn streak. But when two stubborn objects collide, the victory goes to the one with the overall advantage, and the mother was eventually able to drag her animated and sobbing child away from the scene.

That uncomfortable scene provides a nice metaphor for all of life. Life is going to move you along whether you want to move or not. If you decide to dig your heels in, remember that life has an infinitely greater physical and metaphysical advantage. It will twist, stretch, contort, and rip you apart, and once you've been beaten up, you will still get dragged away – just like a child dragged away from a toy store.

That little story also offers a metaphor for the role attachment plays in suffering, and how a detached perspective makes change easier. If you can step back and release your attachment to a given state of affairs, an idea, an object of desire, or an emotion, you are ready and able to change. As long as you are (childishly) attached to a specific thing, to "the way things are," changes to it will have you kicking and screaming.

It's your perspective about something that determines how mentally tough and resilient you will be, and how much suffering you will experience, when that thing starts to change. If, for example, you believe the familiarity of your neighborhood is what makes you safe, then you will feel vulnerable when your street begins to change.

You also have a perspective about "change" itself. Do you endure change, or do you relish it? Do you see change as hard? Or is change an opportunity? You might hold the perspective that change is inevitable, necessary, even welcome, or you might view change as undesirable, something to resist. Change is the only true constant – but change is what you make it. You can lead change, allow it to carry you along, or you can fight it.

If you can achieve a sense of detachment toward change, and adopt a positive perspective toward it, you will be much tougher mentally. But mental toughness isn't only a result of the willingness to change, but, conversely, mental toughness also causes you to be more willing to change. Those who are not strong mentally fear what they do not know, and therefore fear change. The more you embrace and experience change, the stronger your mind becomes, because you see that change is nothing to be afraid of. In fact, change is the preferred state of existence for the mind and body.

It can be fun to think about making changes as long as they're intangible. It's easy to talk about change, to imagine all the things we'd change in our lives, but, when the time comes to actually change, we hesitate, recoil, reconsider, or freeze in indecision. If you are even a little like that, just

45

know that there is nothing wrong with you. You are naturally wired that way, but you can become more comfortable with change. (Mentally tough people aren't born. They are made, one synapse at a time.)

At the same time, it's also natural for us to want change and novelty, but we hesitate because the status quo is comfortable. It's safe. Remember the saying, "Better the devil you know than the angel you don't." It's easy to find yourself at a juncture where your desire to change conflicts with your hesitation, creating a debilitating state of indecision. You are unhappy where you are, but unable to move forward.

It's easy enough to fantasize about changing when you can imagine moving the pieces around effortlessly in your head, without thought, fear, or consequence. "Wouldn't it be nice to move to Paris?" "Wouldn't it be nice to do yoga every day?" Yet, when the time comes to act, you realize that the change will spill over into other areas, with unintended consequences or disrupting other routines. "If I move to Paris, I'll have to learn a new language, and who has time for that?" "Yoga? I am too old to do Yoga. What happens if I sprain my back or something?"

It's true, of course, changes in one part of your life won't remain confined to it. Any change will almost certainly spill over into other areas, and things that do work well can be affected. But unexpected areas that haven't been working may also change for the better.

If you regularly give in to the reluctance to change, over time, you can create a perpetual aversion to embarking on new things, and become resistant to change. "You can't teach an old dog new tricks." Avoiding new things can become the norm. Remember that a stubborn unwillingness to change is the opposite of mental toughness.

There are things you can do to help rid yourself of the fear of change:

1. Start small with incremental steps.
2. Decide to "Do whatever it takes."
3. Adopt a different perspective on change.

You need to get used to change, and one way to do that is to make changes incrementally, in small steps. When the effort you put in, and the effect it has is small enough, making a change won't be experienced as so jarring. It also gives you a chance to experience the impact that changing one thing might have on other areas of your life, so you can be more comfortable with that.

Another way to get used to change is to make lots of little changes regularly. When it becomes just another normal part of the day to do something a little different here and there, change itself becomes normal and familiar. You can even create a habit of looking for something new to try or something to do in different way – every day.

If you have many failed attempts at making changes in your past, or you haven't even tried in a while, it might have become hard to initiate change. Deep down, you already "know" that you are "full of it," and that the endeavor isn't going to amount to anything. You can feel that you'd just be wasting resources to even bother trying.

If that's the case, you'll need to prove to yourself that you can make the changes you have to, and you do that by starting small. When you start small, you get to outcomes faster. The more often you get to experience a benefit from changing, the more you'll begin to believe in the wisdom of acting on your schemes and ideas.

Sometimes, you might need to push yourself a little to get over your reluctance to change. Adopting the attitude and mantra of "Do whatever it takes" can start the momentum going in a new direction. (Remember an object at rest tends to stay at rest.)

Almost two decades ago, needing something to read during a flight, I spotted a little booklet on a small newsstand rack. Less than a hundred pages, I had read that little book cover to cover by the time the flight attendant had completed the safety briefing. By the time we landed, I had read the book eight more times. I still read that book at least once a year. The entire book can be distilled down to just one line, "Do whatever it takes."

The key is that if you decide you want something, then you do whatever it takes to do it. For it to be effective, you need to tell yourself, "Do whatever it takes," before you even start. All too often, we tell ourselves we want something, but when we get to the hard part, we give up, decide the cost is too high, or have a change of heart. Inertia and the momentum of the way things are makes it easier to do what you have always done, so that extra "push" can make all the difference.

Commit to "Do whatever it takes." You will find that making any change takes on a whole new meaning when you commit to doing all that it takes to see it through.

Finally, more than anything else, you need to change your perspective toward change itself. Your attitude toward change can be the determining factor in how change will affect you. If you think change is difficult – it will certainly live up to your expectations. If you look forward to change with anticipation and excitement – you can enjoy the new experiences it brings.

Being willing to change can be one of the hardest things for people, and there will always be areas where it is more difficult than in others. If you are dogmatic, exacting, methodical, or you have an obsession, it can be even harder. But change is an integral part of life, and the more comfortable you are with it, the better.

Ultimately, being flexible and open to change is a requirement for genuine mental toughness. It's not true mental toughness, if you are only mentally strong when things are going the way you expect them to, the way you are used to, or when you aren't faced with challenges.

Chapter 5: Ready for Challenges

The corollary of being flexible and willing to change is being ready to face challenges. Being able to assess the situation, process the incoming stimuli, and roll with the punches is an important component of mental toughness. If you expect life to always be smooth, you won't achieve emotional stability and mental toughness, because you won't be able to deal with the unexpected. And you can always expect the unexpected.

If you expect that there will be bumps along the road, you can bounce with them. If you have both emotional stability and the flexibility to change, then you are ready to face any challenge along the way. If you adopt the perspective that challenges are neither good nor bad, they just are, and take a detached perspective from them, you will be more able to see them for what they are, and deal with them as just another part of your day.

The Stoic philosopher, Marcus Aurelius, wrote in his *Meditations* that one should rise each morning telling themselves that someone will offend them during the course of the day, someone will want something from them at some point in the day, and that one needs to fortify themselves against this. He writes about starting his mornings by preparing his mind for the onslaught of irritations, problems, and frustrations that could be in store for the day.

You don't need to psych yourself out thinking about all the troubles that could be in store for you, but you can mentally ready yourself to face challenges that may come your way. You can fortify yourself emotionally before your day has even started. It will set your perspective for the day and establish a basis for emotional stability.

A big part of mental toughness is being able to withstand otherwise unexpected negative events. It is the thing you are least expecting that can knock you off your game. You need to strike a balance between fearing something and preparing for something. Mental toughness is built on understanding that it is normal to encounter challenges that you will have to overcome.

Having said that, there is a subset of people who seem to manifest the things that they worry about. For them, being at the ready to deal with unwanted circumstances is almost like leaving a light on for unwanted trouble to knock on their door.

Remember, being at the ready is a very different thing than attracting unwanted events to yourself, as a kind of self-fulfilling prophecy. If you start focusing on the things that arouse the greatest emotional response as you prepare yourself to face unforeseen events, that will invite your imagination to run wild. If you have a negative mindset and perspective, your tendency will be to raise negative issues emotionally, creating an affinity and predisposition for them. So, as you prepare yourself for whatever could happen, you may end up attracting those very things to happen. Instead of staving them off, you are waving them in. If that describes you, detachment will be your biggest ally.

When you are readying yourself for the challenges you may encounter in your day, a stance of detachment is critical. You do not want to attach yourself to the worry and anticipation of negative outcomes. Mental toughness comes from being able to "see" problems, without becoming immersed and attached to them. A detached perspective provides the "cool head" that distinguishes individuals who become known for handling crises well, for being mentally tough.

One thing, in particular, will help you be ready to deal with whatever may come, and that is being healthy and physically fit. Confidence in your own ability to handle anything that comes your way, feeling ready to pull the trigger at any instant, comes from a feeling of mental and physical fitness. The mental strength of being feeling prepared comes from physical strength as well as mental focus. If you walk or run every day, your mind will stay well-primed, focused, and ready for anything.

It is impossible to be at your best mental fitness if you are not physically fit. No matter how much you reflect and do mental exercises, if you are sedentary, not getting enough exercise and sunlight, you aren't going to be in the best mental shape – which is a definite prerequisite to mental toughness.

Because the mind is a function of the brain, it cannot exceed its abilities. The brain is the physical organ inside your skull. It is as tangible as your heart or your kidneys. Therefore, the mind excels when it is fed tangible nutrients, energy, and oxygen, as well as the intangible, knowledge, ideas, sensory experiences, and thinking challenges.

Your mind is not physical at all. It is a concept that arises from the existence of the physical brain. There is no other organ in the body that creates an intangible manifestation of itself the way the brain creates its own idea of the mind. However, your mind is what you experience and what you make of it – your brain is merely tissue, fed by a constant and voluminous amount of energy and oxygen.

Nevertheless, your mental toughness relies on the efficient physical functioning of your brain. The fact is that your brain is a resource hog. While the brain is only 2 percent of the weight of the entire body, it uses more than 20 percent of the oxygen and 20 percent of the energy used by the entire body does. In fact, the body prioritizes brain function in distributing resources, even though the brain burns calories at a faster rate than any other system or organ in the body. Intense concentration can tire you out, make you hungry, and burn calories just as much as any workout.

In particular, working out physically increases brain function, increases the brain's motivation to accomplish what it sets out to do, and releases hormones that are important to mental toughness, resiliency, and overall functioning.

Here is something to try that'll show you just how much of an impact working out can have on your readiness to go after what you want (or act on any other kind of contingency). Start by setting a modest goal for something that you want. (This goal isn't one that has anything to do with physical fitness.) If you haven't been exercising regularly, do a fifteen minute workout, just enough to break a sweat and get the circulation going, as you think about your goal or objective. If you are a regular gym visitor, do your regular workout while visualizing your goal.

If you do this for a while, you will find yourself feeling a growing affinity for your goal, because your mind has been releasing positive neurotransmitters during your workout which have become associated with that goal. Those neurotransmitters increase positive emotional associations in your memory and results in a greater attraction toward your goal. It almost puts you on autopilot to achieve what you want.

In the context of mental toughness, exercise fortifies your mind so that you are constantly ready to achieve your goals and desires, focused, and less likely to be distracted. With a healthy body, and a consequently healthy mind, you will be ready to face and overcome challenges. A large part of the strength of mental toughness is simply being ready for whatever may come.

Chapter 6: Strength

In many respects, everything in this book can be considered a "strength" that contributes to mental toughness. In addition, of course, there are those strengths (capabilities and traits) that are your own unique advantages and personal assets, things that make you singularly effective. But before we look at those kinds of strengths, we'll talk about strength in its other meaning.

"Strength" can refer to the amount of stress, pressure, strain, or force that something (or someone) can withstand – or offer against something else. That relates to durability, endurance, and power. We have already talked about flexibility (and the willingness to change) as being one component of that type of strength, that is, of the ability to withstand stress.

It must be noted that true strength of this kind, being strong mentally, is not the same as putting on a show of strength. The person who only makes an outward display of strength may be able to appear strong on days when there is no stress. However, the moment that stress increases and becomes overwhelming, that external show of strength breaks down.

On the other hand, a person who has genuine internal strength and isn't wasting effort on projecting an appearance of strength, is able to handle a crisis and stress better. There is mental capacity to spare when it isn't wasted on maintaining an act or defending an image.

There is a saying, "Still waters run deep." Strength that runs deep below the surface reveals itself in the face of adversity and stress. But strength that is projected onto the surface evaporates as soon as stress is applied to that superficial image.

Mental toughness is about inner strength. It's not about huge muscles, chiseled biceps, or the biggest guns. As Theodore Roosevelt, the longest serving American President and mentally tough despite ill health and being crippled by polio, once said, "Speak softly and carry a big stick." While tin-pot dictators may flex their muscles with military parades, this is not what we mean by the kind of strength that contributes to mental toughness.

When someone starts trying to show off how strong they are, that is usually a sure sign that important weaknesses are being masked and that there isn't any real strength there. Generally, the most powerful people are also the most reserved about displaying their power. Humility has its own kind of strength to add into the mix.

The strength of mental toughness isn't about brute strength or aggression. Someone who is typically quick to anger and ready to throw a punch or express disagreement through physical force reveals a limited internal strength. That kind of behavior is driven more by ego preservation or by one of the many fears that reside in the primal part of the brain.

While tin-pot dictators everywhere in the world have come and gone, the quiet, understated strength of mentally tough leaders like Martin Luther King and Mahatma Gandhi, who stood up against overwhelming forces to change history, continue to inspire millions to their causes. Brute strength may put a dictator ahead of the game at first, but eventually every one of them, from Stalin to Hitler, to Pol Pot and Idi Amin, all have ended up on the ash heap of history.

So, where does that powerful inner strength come from? That kind of inner strength and mental toughness comes from having the confidence of knowing who you are, what you believe (your perspective), and your own personal strengths – and being able to rely on them.

For the moment, set aside your concerns for your weaknesses. Instead, this is about identifying what your strengths are, doing more of them, building them up, and buttressing your mental toughness with them. When you know you have a particular strength, talent, or capability that you can rely on, it provides you not only with a reserve of confidence and power to draw from when you need to be mentally tough, but also specific capabilities you can call upon in situations of stress or crisis. In other words, knowing your own personal "strengths" contributes to your inner strength.

To identify your own personal "strengths," don't just write a list of what you think they are or of things that you think you're good at. You don't want a list of what you automatically think of, and you don't want to overstate or underestimate your abilities either.

Instead, to dig deeper and assess your strengths more accurately, look back to times you overcame challenges, when you "won" at something. Perhaps you got a promotion at work because you did your job exceptionally well. Were you accepted into university because you excelled academically? Maybe you built a birdhouse. Make a list of things you consider victories or accomplishments. List things you were praised for, rewarded for, felt good about, and so on. Look for times you vanquished obstacles, and look at what it took to get there. Also, look at the desires you've had in your life, and list the ones you've achieved – a hobby, a family, a house, a car, a good job, an education.

Now comes the important part of the exercise. Dig into each victory or accomplishment on your list and look for the specific underlying strengths and abilities you had to demonstrate to achieve it.

What did you do differently from situations where you (or others) didn't succeed? You'll find patterns emerging. There will also be things so natural and easy for you that you take them for granted. Maybe you are really good at persuading skeptics face-to-face. It could be that you produce outstanding work when you spend extra time organizing it beforehand. You'll be surprised by the strengths you have that you never even realized were there.

Use that list to make better choices, doing what is most aligned with your personal strengths. It might suggest new directions you hadn't thought of before. Working from your strengths will always be more powerful, moving you forward faster than struggling through weaknesses. It'll waste less mental resources, and it'll keep you in your mental toughness zone.

Understanding your own unique "strengths" is really the first step toward self-awareness, which is the topic of the next chapter.

Chapter 7: Self-awareness

We've been talking about identifying your own personal strengths in the last chapter, so you are already well on your way to greater self-awareness. Self-awareness goes hand in hand with having mental strength and toughness. It's hard to imagine someone without self-knowledge or self-awareness as being mentally tough.

This chapter won't focus on understanding your personal strengths so much as just becoming more self-aware generally, and on understanding your own way of getting in and out of difficulties. Ultimately, you need to understand as much as you can about yourself, your strengths, and weaknesses, if you are going to be mentally tough.

Self-awareness normally comes with age, wisdom, and experience, but you don't have to wait, if you learn the art of observation and reflection. The kind of self-awareness that normally takes a lifetime of experiences to acquire can be yours with observation and reflection.

Reflection was offered up in Chapter 2 as a technique for developing greater detachment and perspective. A regular practice of reflection is equally valuable (even crucial) for gaining self-awareness.

There is another useful and easy technique for self-reflection that you can use to better understand yourself (or any situation). You can use it to uncover hidden issues, unexpected connections between things, and hidden motives. Do this exercise on your own in writing or partner up with another person who can ask the questions. It's a good technique to add to your repertoire of journaling exercises.

The exercise uses a framework of "Why?" questions. The answers gradually reveal what isn't readily apparent on the surface, including contradictions.

Identify an issue about yourself that you want to understand better, and start asking, "Why?" Each time you have an answer, ask "Why?" of that answer, creating a chain of questions and answers.

1. Why?
2. Why?
3. Why?
4. Why?
5. Why?

Each time you ask "Why?" you peel away another layer to reveal another set of hidden causes until you find a root cause. Keep going until you feel you've exhausted the issue by experiencing an "Aha!" or just reaching the bottom of the issue.

For example, perhaps you just paid a regular bill late again, even though you had the money. You could start by asking yourself, "I paid this bill late. Why?" and quietly allowing an answer to arise from within. If the answer is "I don't like paying that bill," the next question naturally is, "Why don't I like paying this bill?" Perhaps the answer is, "I feel that I might need that money for an emergency." That leads to the next question, "Why do I feel I'll need money for an emergency?" Any number of answers could emerge from that, leading into the next question, and so forth.

By the time you have get to the bottom of the matter, you realize you need a certain amount of financial cushion to feel safe. In other words, you have been paying that bill late because paying it arouses a feeling of insecurity instilled by a childhood of poverty. Seeing all the elements of the issue laid out so clearly makes it easier to understand (and forgive yourself for). A solution might also become obvious, just from doing the exercise, as in the next example.

A close friend's son was once suspended for cheating in school. His parents were livid and confused. Things weren't progressing toward a solution, so they asked me to help. I knew the boy to be intelligent, sharp witted, and quick to pick up things. Together, we went through the Why?

questions, and found the root problem within an hour, plain to see.

It turned out he'd been getting bad headaches and hadn't been able to keep up with his usual workload. He hadn't wanted to worry his parents, or let them down, so he started to get help from friends. One thing led to another, and he got caught. Within a week of going through the exercise, his eyes were checked, and corrective lenses prescribed. Within six weeks, he was back at the top of his class.

Doing the Why? exercise can not only help identify solutions for problems, it can give you a lot of insight into yourself. In particular, it can really help you understand how you find yourself having problems with undesirable consequences.

Of course, we all have problems, but some have more than others. Some people are habitual problem magnets, perpetually under the shadow of a storm cloud, while others seem to walk between the raindrops even in a heavy downpour. Which are you? If you tend to be a problem magnet, or even have one troublesome repetitive pattern, you can add the next exercise to your toolbox for understanding yourself better.

We each have unique paths we take to arrive at problems, whether they are major crises or insignificant irritations. We all do something that leads to something else which intersects with chance – and comes back to us dressed as a problem. Problems don't materialize in a vacuum. They have identifiable sources and workable solutions.

How you deal with a problem once you find yourself there depends on your attitude. In this exercise, you can use your problem as an opportunity to gain self-awareness and learn how you arrived at it.

The goal of this exercise is to retrace your steps to identify what set you on the path to the problem and turning points along the way. Adopt a detached perspective, and starting with the problem, look back, retracing the sequence of steps along the way. You will find a path paved with events, actions, reactions, errors, assumptions, and chance interventions.

Whatever your well-trod path is, you are really looking for the most common recurring elements. That path is unique to you. It takes a little time, but, eventually, you can trace that path, and the key moments along it.

Take, for example, a person who constantly loses his job. He goes from one job to the next, sometimes within a few weeks. Upon reflection, he may realize that he has a habit of getting into arguments with his superiors, making it difficult for him to work there. With that, he has a clue into the problem, but doesn't yet have a solution.

If, the next time he gets into a problem with his superiors, he recognizes that the next step will be to lose another job, he stands at a juncture, able to look back to see how he arrived at that point, and where it will lead. That's a valuable vantage point from which to observe.

From that position, he may see that the usual reason he has gotten into problems with his superiors has been overpromising on his deliverables and underdelivering on his promises. He knows he has meant well, but that hasn't been producing good results. The next time he is in that situation, at that turning point, he can look forward and see that he is about to overpromise, but, with the benefit of hindsight, he can choose to do something different, taking a different path for different results.

In the same way, you can trace backward through the prequels of your actions, examining the path you took to arrive at any particular outcome (even the good ones – so you can repeat those). For most of us, those paths will be ones we have taken again and again.

Your first step in identifying how you keep arriving at the same problem outcome is to identify that path. Retrace it back to the start, identifying all the elements that make up the path. Knowing where the path to the problem starts, you will find it easier to change what you do in the future at that critical decision point.

Sometimes the decisive moment is a reaction you've had that's born out of poor perception or out of an unproductive perspective. Other times, you may react out of habit. Habitual responses can seem uncontrollable, getting away from you in a hurry. Like a rapid reflex, it's out the door, before you've had a chance to consider whether it's the right response. Taking a detached perspective to retrace your steps can give that opportunity to reconsider your responses.

The answer isn't to stop having rapid reflexes. The answer is for those rapid responses to be the best ones available. For example, if something was coming right at you at high speed, you'd instinctively duck for cover. That's a reflex you want to have. The alternative is to get hit by the projectile. Instead, what if your response was to raise your arms to protect your face when a high-speed projectile comes at you? So, you raise your arms instead of ducking. Would that be a better option? That would depend on what the high-speed projectile is.

Those are the kinds of questions that you can't process in the middle of the situation, but you should certainly look at it, later, with hindsight, and learn about yourself from your actions.

Every day, we do and say things that are like breadcrumbs that can lead us to discover valuable information about ourselves. If you follow these breadcrumbs, they can lead you to a deeper understanding of yourself, and that self-awareness, in turn, will increase your mental toughness.

Chapter 8: Self-Validation

Self-awareness and self-validation go hand in hand, and together form a solid basis for mental toughness. You need to be self-aware and know who you and what your strengths are in order to have genuine self-validation. Self-validation is the feeling of having internal confirmation of the legitimacy of your own identity.

While it is great to get recognition from others, and it can even help you "see" your own strengths and successes, external validation should always be subservient to internal self-validation. If you depend only on outside validation from others, you can't have true mental toughness, because you will always be vulnerable to not having that external validation.

There are a lot of different ways to try to get validation from outside of yourself. Have you ever come across a person who will do just about anything for someone else? Often that person just wants to be liked, to be validated by someone else. Other people base their view of themselves on the marks they get at school, the approval of teachers, awards they win, or on some other external measure. The list of possibilities is truly endless, whereas internal self-validation is found in only one place, in oneself.

A lot of people work to project an impression to get feedback that validates the image they want to have of themselves. Someone who wants to look like a millionaire might take out a huge loan to buy an expensive car. Seeing other's admiring looks fulfills how they want to see themselves – without the real-world accomplishment to match. Meantime, many of the real millionaires-next-door quietly drive around fully paid older models while banking the money they save, confident in the strength of their financial position, and secure in their self-validation.

Relying on others for validation will never produce genuine mental toughness. It can only ever result in a simulacrum, an image of mental toughness. It's a true point of weakness. The more you mold yourself into what you think others see in you, the more it weakens you. If there is no legitimate internal basis to back up the image, it can collapse at any time. This is the fundamental weakness of both the genuine fraud and the person who just feels like an imposter.

Relying on others or on external sources for self-validation means that you are attached to those externals, instead of relying on your own internal knowing of who you are. You don't have control over those externals, and so you invite suffering and misery by being too attached to external validators, which can fail you. Anyone who has struggled looking for the approval of a parent that is never forthcoming understands the misery and weakness it brings. Perhaps even more importantly, being too attached to external sources of validation makes it harder to achieve detachment, a required ability for maintaining mental toughness.

Having a proven experience of self-reliance is a powerful form of self-validation. Many cultures offer this to their children as a coming-of-age ritual to mark their passage into adulthood. Some people find ways to have these kinds of confidence-building experiences for themselves, even as adults. For others, survival challenges are a form of therapy that allows them to confidently turn their lives around, by validating for themselves what they are capable of. When you know that you can look after yourself, you gain the confidence and self-validation of your own abilities.

Many tribes of the Amazon rainforest have such tests of self-reliance. Boys are given a knife and sent into the jungle without any companion. By the time they are 12, these boys have been in the jungle dozens of times on hunting trips, and foraging for food. When they go into the jungle on their own, there is only one thing left to learn, and that is self-reliance.

Self-reliance offers the greatest form of self-validation there is. It comes when you know you have what it takes to do what is needed to get what you need. Most of the boys who enter the jungle return to the village, after three days of staying safe and foraging for sustenance, with the confidence of a man.

Both boys and girls can leave as a child and return from a challenging experience as an adult. Showing themselves that they can do anything, especially away from their parents, alters the circuitry of the mind.

In the western world, youths don't go into the jungle for three days, but they do go away to college for several years and come back as adults. Granted, they are older, but the effect is less about the academics than proving the ability to survive in their world, away from their parent's protection. *Once you fend for yourself, the world changes.* It is the ultimate form of mental toughness when you know that you can rely on yourself.

Every time you set yourself a goal or challenge and accomplish something you haven't previously done, it is the strongest form of validation, one that you give yourself. It's not about whether someone else tells you how good you are – it is about you knowing that you managed to do something on your own.

Self-validation doesn't just happen once in your life – it's a continuous process. The boy who goes out into the jungle and comes back a man is expected to become part of the tribe's hunting party and to travel the paths of the jungle alone if needed. In the same way, once you accomplish something that validates your identity and abilities to yourself, you should not stop there. You need to keep doing it, repeatedly, and at higher degrees of complexity.

Self-validation is about strengthening your mind by proving to yourself that you can get the task done. This is the reason children are encouraged to start with something small and accomplish that before they are given a more complex task. It's not about how big an accomplishment is – it's about how many little accomplishments, and how frequently, you can pull them off. For instance, ten small accomplishments are significantly better than a single major one in the long run.

It's as if there is a self-validation tank in each of us. That tank needs to be constantly added to, without regard for the size of what you put into it. If you only contribute one huge win, after a short while, that self-validation withers away, like the caricature of the high school football star who pathetically relives the "win" of the big game, but never claims any other victories in life. But if you can fill that tank with fresh self-validations on a daily or weekly basis, then that tank is not only going to remain filled up, but it is also going to fuel your forward momentum.

Self-validation isn't simply telling yourself positive things in a mirror – you need to make sure to do things you can succeed at. Remember it's about putting accomplishments in the tank, and using that as fuel for the next accomplishment. Over time, this leads to huge gains and gives you the momentum to advance in other areas of your life.

One good way to do this on a daily basis is to pack your schedule in the mornings with little successes so that by the time you get to the middle of the morning, you have the energy and motivation to do even bigger things as the day goes on.

Take baby steps.

Self-validation is a unique phenomenon. When you start out, try to rapidly accumulate smaller successes, and quickly ramp those up in frequency and magnitude. The faster you manufacture a "hit," the more you feel the self-validation. That will start tuning your mind for success.

Pretty soon, you begin to ooze confidence. That aura of confidence is enough to help you succeed at other things beyond what is on the list you began with. When frequent and relentless, the self-validation process and the successful outcomes of tasks and objectives feed on each other until they reach critical mass.

Eventually, success, itself, becomes a habit. When you use self-validation as a reward for success, that reward is reliable and highly effective, in a way that no external reward can be. It's the difference between being intrinsically or extrinsically motivated. Intrinsic motivation is the result of self-validation as the reward for success, and it will carry you forward long past the motivation offered by any external reward or validation. The truly successful in any field are always intrinsically motivated by their own self-validation.

Self-validation isn't about making affirmations, but affirmations do have their place in getting you into the state you want to be in, a state that makes it easier to do the things necessary to succeed and achieve self-validating proof.

Instead, self-validation is practical, requiring consistent action. Doing something successfully today without repeating it again for weeks is not as effective. Instead, fight daily for small successes – and larger ones if possible. Make it a point to find something to chalk up as a "win" every day. When you do that, self-validation becomes a powerful pillar of increased mental toughness.

The flip side and result of self-validation is taking responsibility. By definition, self-validation means that you know you are responsible for who you are and what you have done. Taking responsibility is part of being mentally tough. Making excuses, avoiding responsibility, not doing what is needed – none of these things describe someone who exhibits mental toughness.

That sense of responsibility tends to spread out to broader areas. Mentally tough people get up and do something about the things that bother them, instead of wasting energy complaining. They tend to participate in their societies to make a difference where they can. They help others without being overwhelmed by it. Mentally tough people do not allow things to affect them; they affect things around them. Mentally tough people are the first to take responsibility for whatever happens in their wider orbit.

Successful people who are self-validating start to look outward at changing the world. Their horizons become significantly larger than the average guy, because they know internally what they are capable of, without needing external validation to give them permission. Successful people just move forward and take responsibility for making their visions into a reality. Bill Gates wanted a computer in every home in the world, and Jeff Bezos wanted to create a marketplace that would sell to everyone. Mental toughness is a requirement for being able to achieve such extreme levels of success and achievement.

A sense of responsibility is also usually related to having a well-defined moral compass. Mentally tough people who know who they are and have a sense of responsibility for what they do don't generally need to use morally questionable means to achieve their ends.

Although there are other ways to achieve coherence, having a well-defined moral code is one particularly powerful way to create a coherent character that pulls together the various elements that make up mental toughness.

A strong moral code is built from within yourself. Something inside you tells you that a thing is wrong to do. Something inside you tells you that doing an act will serve the greater good. A strong moral code comes from your own instincts – and knowing who you really are. Your moral values reveal what you value. For example, if you value life, killing another human being would be against your moral values. Instinctively, you know that not understanding the value of life would have a long-term effect on you.

A mentally tough person has a well-defined moral code that binds virtues together and provides coherence in daily life. That moral code is the natural result of self-awareness of what is valued combined with the sense of responsibility that self-validation fosters.

Chapter 9: Focus

When we imagine a person that we'd describe as being mentally tough, we are very likely to imagine someone who is very focused, that is, someone who is in control of directing their own attention.

Before we start talking about ways to improve focus, let's first consider the role that focus plays in perspective. As we've already discussed, the ability to control your perspective, how you "see" things, is at the heart of mental toughness. And what you focus on has everything to do with what your perspective is at that moment.

How do you change your perspective? You change your focus. Just as changing the focus on a camera will change the perspective on what you "see," changing your mental focus will change your perspective, point-of-view, and filter on what you think and experience.

A well-known cognitive optical illusion is a perfect metaphor for the way that focus controls what you "see" – in other words, how focus changes your perspective, and, thus, what you "see." If you do an internet search for "Rubin vase," you will find a variety of versions of ambiguous, reversing, bi-stable images that appear to be different things depending on your focus. Look at a Rubin vase image in one way, and you will see a vase centered in the foreground of the image. Focus differently, and the background suddenly becomes foreground, revealing the profiles of two faces looking at each other. The "take-away" is that what you focus on changes what you see.

It is also virtually impossible to really see both at the same time. If you try, you'll find yourself having to switch back and forth rapidly between perspectives, but you won't truly be able to hold both at the same time. That, too, is an important metaphor for the importance of controlling what you focus on, because you can deliberately or inadvertently become "blind" to things – a natural feature of focus and perspective that can both work for you and against you.

As the Rubin vase so aptly illustrates, controlling what you focus on is a powerful and necessary tool in your arsenal of mental skills that contributes to your level of mental toughness. Deciding what to focus on is an important element of effective focus.

Taking a moment of detachment can be the simplest and best way to get the chance to consciously decide what to focus on, rather than being distracted willy-nilly by everything going on. Practicing detachment, which we have already talked a lot about, helps with focus, by making it easier not to get swept up by distractions. The STOPP technique (Chapter 3) doesn't need to be reserved for emotionally overwhelming situations. It can also be used when your attention is overwhelmed, making it difficult to direct your focus.

Most of the time, there is a lot to process at once. In a world beset by multi-tasking, we expect our conscious mind to multi-task, forgetting that it wasn't designed for that. There is a sort of parallel processing going on in our brain, but only some of it is conscious. The rest is subconscious. It is more effective to have the conscious mind focus on doing just one thing – while allowing the subconscious to do everything else.

The brain operates on several different frequencies. Some functions of the brain occur at slower or faster speeds than others. The reason you aren't aware of your brain's subconscious activities is that they occur at different frequencies than those in your conscious awareness. Like a radio that can only tune into one station at a time, this relieves you of the chaos that would result from being aware of everything that your brain does. That would be like having every radio station playing at once, and not being able to select one to listen to.

Meanwhile, many things are going on around you at the speed of life, that is, the speed of things moving in the physical world. There are maximum speeds that the conscious senses can detect and make sense of. Magic and illusion occur at speeds just outside of the limited ranges of what is detectable by human senses.

An analogy might be helpful to illustrate the brain's response to all the input coming at it, and how that affects focus.

Imagine a waterfall about two feet wide, dropping from a high cliff. There is a cave opening behind the waterfall with a railway track running out of it, like the ones used in old mines. Now, imagine a string of mining carts (also two feet wide) coming out of the cave, through the waterfall, moving at the perfect speed to capture all of the water falling from the cliff into those mining carts.

Now, suppose that the rate of water falling speeds up while the speed of the carts remains the same. What will happen? The water would fill up the carts and then overflow, wouldn't it? Anything exceeding the speed of the carts would be too much for the carts to hold.

The human mind is a little like those mining carts, moving at a specific speed. Meanwhile, the world is moving at a variety of speeds. Some things move so slowly they are undetectable without special tools, like the growth of a tree or a seed, while other things move so fast, like light, that we can't see the movement. However, most human creations, from cars to conversations, fall within the range that mimics the speed of the conscious mind – the speed of the mining carts. As long as there is just one stream coming at it at the right speed, the conscious mind can catch all of it.

The subconscious mind operates much faster, and, metaphorically speaking, can capture a lot more water pouring down the cliff. Not only does it catch what the conscious mind misses, it also catches additional things that the conscious mind is not able to. If you have faith that your subconscious mind is capturing everything that's necessary, there is really no reason to overwhelm your conscious mind trying to focus consciously on everything at once.

Focus is simply about giving your conscious mind only one task to attend to and allowing it to ignore everything else.

However, even when you aren't trying to do too many things at once, your conscious mind still takes in and processes a lot of unnecessary data – which means there may not be enough room left in that mining cart for what you actually want it to carry.

It is natural for your mind to be occupied with some things. Safety, for instance. You need to stay on the alert for things that could jeopardize your safety or the safety of your belongings. The more you have to be concerned about, the more of your mind is preoccupied with staying safe.

If you are sitting in a coffee shop, trying to work on your laptop, part of you is going to be conscious of your bag on the seat beside you. If you were to focus 100 percent on what you are working on, you may forget to keep an eye on that bag.

A better way to stay focused on what you want to is to put yourself into a situation where you don't need to keep an eye out for dangers. It's the difference between falling asleep in the safety and comfort of your own home versus falling asleep in the park. At home, you can sleep as deeply as you need to for a proper rest. In the park, you always need to keep yourself partially alert to stay safe.

You can easily stop those types of distractions from demanding your attention. You just need be somewhere that minimizes those considerations. Go into a room, get the temperature comfortable, lock the doors so that you are safe, and block out the sounds of the outside world. Also turn off your iPod and TV, so there are no entertaining temptations competing for your attention.

Distractions are anything that takes your attention away from the one thing you need to focus on. Even things that need to be done can be distractions, if they have your attention at the wrong time, that is, when you are trying to do something else. If you need to do a math problem, but you start thinking about a history question – that's a distraction.

There is an easy trick for dealing with that last type of distraction. When you have a task that you want to devote singular attention to, have a "distraction notebook" handy on the side. Whenever you think of something you need to do or have an unrelated idea, and your attention is being drawn away from what you are dedicated to doing, jot that task or idea down in a running list in that notebook. Then, you can let the distraction go, knowing that you won't forget it because it's safely tucked away in that notebook, and you can bring your focus right back to where you want it.

Developing focus is much easier when you understand what it really is. If you want to focus on something, just make sure that you don't do anything else. While that sounds simple and intuitive, it is not always easy to do because of the habits you have picked up along the way.

Anything that isn't related to what you are doing is a distraction, and distractions produce a confused mind. Clarity of focus means less confusion. A clear mind is a strong mind. Not knowing or comprehending something is not the same thing as being confused. A person who is often confused would never be described as mentally tough.

Allowing yourself to become distracted and confused is a habit – a habit you need to break. That's right. Confusion is a habit, no different from any other habit, even smoking.

85

Habits, both good and bad ones, are made up of three elements, trigger, act, and reward. The trigger creates an urge to do an act. Taking that action (external or internal) generates a reward in the brain when pleasure neurotransmitters are released. That makes you feel good for doing the act, and it reinforces the habit, a sequence of trigger and act.

Each time you give in to a distraction, taking your focus away from what you are doing, you are rewarded. Remember, the brain is a pretty smart economist. It can calculate the return on a task against the effort required, and, if it doesn't see the benefit, it is going to reward you for not doing it.

Remember that focus takes a lot of energy. The brain's default position is to avoid focusing on things that are hard to figure out or difficult to understand. If something difficult is important, and the end justifies the effort, then you will need to override that natural tendency, and get out of the habit of letting yourself become distracted.

If you find the prospect of focusing on a single thing overwhelming, get a timer, and set it for a manageable length of time during which you will focus. Knowing that the allotted time is not endless, and that you will be able to take an attention "break" can ease the anxiety that trying to stay focused for extended periods of time can sometimes cause. The timer can also be used to gradually build up the ability to focus for longer periods.

Focus is an essential part of mental toughness. It disciplines the mind to stay "on topic" to do what you have decided to do. It also helps maintain the "state" of mind you want to be in and the perspective you want to hold. Focus combined with a positive mindset (in the next chapter) is a powerful combination, one that could almost be called a hallmark of one who is mentally tough.

Chapter 10: Positive Outlook

A positive outlook is truly a requirement for mental toughness. A positive outlook makes a person more resilient and able to cope with the ups and downs of life. It is also known that, having an optimistic attitude, a person is not just happier, but also more creative, more successful, and makes better decisions.

A positive outlook or mindset is the habit of thinking about things positively, maintaining a perspective that sees things in an optimistic and positive light. Having a positive outlook means having a habit of looking for the "silver lining," making the best of any situation, and seeing everything as an opportunity.

And, so, talking about having a positive outlook brings us right back to the topic of perspectives. Things are neither "good" nor "bad" except as perspective makes them so. And our own perspective is something we have much more control over than we generally give ourselves credit for.

Remember that everything we experience through our senses and everything we think is subject to our perspective, filtered and shaped by it. We automatically tend to lump things, events, experiences, and ideas together into one of two piles, positive or negative, good or bad, desirable or undesirable. It's a natural thing, and even essential to basic survival.

We are hard-wired to move toward what is desirable, and away from the undesirable. The "problem" with this process is that the filter (our perspective) through which we sort everything into those two piles doesn't always work to our advantage. It can stop us from moving toward things that would be better for us and keep us from experiencing the "best" of what life has to offer.

There is a third alternative. Remember that detachment is that very special kind of perspective where we pull back into a more neutral zone, neither positive nor negative. Detachment is arguably most important as a meta-perspective that provides a way for us to shift and change our perspective, point of view, and interpretation of things.

Detachment gives you the ability to take control of your own outlook, to make it as positive or negative as you choose. It allows you to pull back from a negative perspective so that you can reframe it into a more positive way of looking at experiences, ideas, etc. Detachment gives you the opportunity to reinterpret things – hopefully, to contribute to a more positive outlook. With the help of detachment, there are always ways to see anything from a more positive perspective.

There are, of course, times when that same detachment is invaluable for seeing problems and negatives clearly, for seeing things "for what they are." Sometimes, you need to reinterpret something to understand that it is undesirable, so that you can change it. Changing what has been holding you back is a very good thing. Detachment makes that easier because it buffers the negative, painful emotions that we all naturally avoid.

As you move through life, you anticipate, through your positive or negative perspective, how things are going to turn out. You can believe that something is going to end well, or that it is going to end poorly. The way you think about it from the outset is important. It often determines the outcome.

A positive outlook can become a self-fulfilling prophecy. Instead of being afraid of all the stumbling blocks you might encounter, you can be solution oriented. Maintaining a positive mindset as you ponder the challenges ahead will help keep you from becoming discouraged, or even losing interest in an endeavor before you even take the first step.

Having a positive outlook is seeing everything that happens in your life as something that contributes to who you are and moves your experience forward. It is as simple as you make it.

Any event can be seen as constructive or destructive, depending on the perspective. Forest fires are automatically thought of as destructive, but, on a net basis, in nature, a forest fire does more good than harm. As it burns everything to the ground, it changes the fertility of the soil so the next crop of trees will be healthy, and without fungal or parasitic infestation.

Pyrophytic plants spontaneously combust, killing nearby plants, reducing them to fertilizer and nutrients. The pyrophytic plant also burns up, but its seeds fall to the ground, covered by a protective layer that shields them from the fire. Once the fire has died out, the seeds crack after the first rain, and new life sprouts and thrives. Life emerges out of apparent destruction. So, which is it really, destructive or constructive?

When you step back to look at life, with all its chaos and order, you don't find good or bad, just continuity and consequences. Continuity is consequences following from causes and causes sparking consequences. All things are connected through cause and effect. Everything that happens is just consequence and continuity – without animus. In the end, it is always only what you make of it.

Having a positive mindset isn't about being Pollyanna or irrationally optimistic when there is nothing to be optimistic about. It's also not about sitting down and doing nothing, falsely believing fortune will fall from the sky. It won't, and that approach will only set you up to be insensitive to what it really means to be positive.

Having a positive mindset allows you to take all things that happen, as a result of your own or someone else's actions or just happenstance, and realize that they are what they are, without any malice toward you. Things happen, and you just have to brush it off. Keep going, and keep trying until what you have envisioned materializes.

This is where mental toughness comes into play. Mental toughness is a state of mind that doesn't rely on conditions having to be "good" and doesn't need to reject the "bad" things.

Success isn't "good" while failure is "bad" – they are simply two sides of the same coin. Even your body wasn't built to have only good things happen to you. You need some "bad" things to trigger growth. To be successful, you need to grow through challenges. In growing, you will face tough times along with easier ones. It may be inconvenient. It may be annoying. It may be embarrassing. It can even be really hard. But is that "bad"?

A mentally tough and resilient positive mindset always expects good to come out of the things that happen – it expects growth out of all things, including what seems, at the time, to be a setback or negative. A positive mindset doesn't simply see bad things as "bad." Instead, it frames them as opportunities or as lessons. There is no advancement and improvement without the discomfort of growth. Hardship challenges you to move out of your comfort zone.

A positive mindset is about more than just feeling good about everything. It also requires logical reasoning. Good and bad things happen as the consequence of other events, following the rules of nature and physics, without hidden agendas. If you run while carrying a glass of milk, you will eventually spill it. A habit of driving recklessly is likely to get you into an accident someday. Even if you drive carefully, someone else driving recklessly may run into you. That another person's actions will inevitably affect you is a consequence of living in a community.

Every event and thing can be looked at with reasoning and logic – and then you can decide, through the perspective you choose to adopt, the meanings you attach to them.

Give a negative person a bar of gold, and they will complain about the weight they have to lug around, but give a positive person dung, and they will be glad to have something to fertilize their plants with.

There are many ways to develop a more positive outlook, and most are straightforward, even common advice. They aren't hidden mysteries –

the only secret is actually doing them. But, at those times that you aren't feeling very positive, it can be hard to think of doing even what's obvious.

1. **Smile.** Even if you don't feel like smiling, the act of smiling signals the brain to release chemicals that will make you feel more positive.

2. **Laugh.** Laughter, even when you don't feel like laughing at first, is a lot like smiling, because it will cause the release of feel-good brain chemicals. It also improves state of mind through its unique breathing patterns. Laughter has long been known to improve health outcomes – "Laughter is the best medicine."
   If you get really serious about adding laughter to your repertoire, you might consider joining (or forming) a Laughter Yoga group that meets early in the morning for the specific purpose of starting the day with vigorous laughter. It's positively contagious.

3. **Get physically active.** Exercise and physical activity are recognized for improving mental outlook and releasing more of those feel-good brain chemicals.

4. **Surround yourself with positivity.** Spend more time with people who have a

positive outlook. Surround yourself with positive images, quotes, and other forms of positive input.

5. **Replace negative self-talk with positive self-talk.** Everyone has a chattering voice in their head. If you notice yourself telling yourself negative things, replace those with positively framed statements as much as possible.

6. **Use positive language to describe yourself and your life.** Emphasize the "can" over the "can't," and the congratulatory over the complaining. Pay attention to the language you use — it might surprise you how much it reveals about your perspective.

7. **Pivot from the negative.** Even though you need to be aware of many negative things, you don't need to dwell on them. Notice what you need to, and then withdraw your attention from it. On balance, direct your attention onto things that are more positive. (Notice the news for what you need to know, but don't drown in it.)

8. **Reframe challenges and obstacles.** When something looks negative, try to see

it from a different perspective. What kind of opportunity does the problem present? Is it really a "good" thing that it happened? Has something good come of it? Were you missing something that you needed to know about?

9. **Keep a "gratitude journal."** If you spend a few moments every day to make a list of things you are grateful for that day, over time, your perspective will naturally shift into a more positive zone.

None of these ideas are new or unusual. But it does take a little bit of focused attention and perseverance to remember to do any of them. The more accustomed you are to a negative momentum, the more effort it will take to remember to do the little things that can shift your outlook to a more positive one. Over time, it does get easier, especially as you find yourself feeling better, and more optimistic.

It takes a certain amount of mental toughness to maintain a positive mindset, to keep it on track. But it also goes the other way. A positive mindset helps to foster mental toughness, nourishing it with resiliency, energy, and motivation. A positive outlook and mental toughness feed off each other.

Chapter 11: Patience

Patience is an important part of having a positive outlook. All things happen in their own time. And it isn't necessarily when we want or expect them to happen.

Our perception of time versus the time it really takes for something to happen can be skewed for a lot of different reasons. Have you ever wanted something so badly that it felt like it took forever? You know, like waiting for something you bought online to arrive that you've wanted for so long? Then, there are other times you don't want something to happen, and you put it off, but suddenly it's right in front of you – like a visit to the dentist for a root canal.

We experience the passing of time filtered through our expectations and perspectives. We expect time passing to feel a certain way. That expectation is the fruit of our perceptions. Those perceptions, in turn, are the products of self-fulfilling expectations of what time passing will feel like.

It is important to remember that our human physiology was never designed to adapt to the timepieces that keep time in the external world, and that can cause all sorts stress, frustration, and anxiety. Einstein postulated that time moves differently for each of us. You might just be right when you experience time as slowing down or speeding up depending on what you are doing, but because we live in a world that needs to be synchronized, we have to readjust our internal clocks to coordinate with the outside world. That means time can become a sticking point. A child's hour of cartoons passes too rapidly, but his hour of chores seems to move like molasses. We've all been there.

Because our physiology doesn't reliably detect the passage of time, it takes a significant amount of mental strength to apply patience to anything. But having patience has a reciprocal relationship with mental strength – it is both cause and consequence. On one hand, applying patience builds mental toughness, and, on the other, mental toughness increases patience.

(This sort of mechanism with reciprocal benefits is common to many aspects of mental toughness. You think you are doing one thing, and the results are going in one direction, but it is really working in both directions, having a compound and resonating effect on your psyche and physiology.)

You need to internalize the practice of patience to be able to control your mind, and it is an important building block for mental toughness. So, what is patience?

Patience can mean a lot of different things to different people, but the one thing it always boils down to is coping with the stress of expectations. We can look at patience in the context of time, you can look at patience in the context of disappointment with an outcome, or you can look at patience in the context of failure. Regardless of how you look at it, the one thing in common is that patience has everything to do with how you handle expectations.

In this age of rapid development and deployment, we tend to rush things, and that becomes a habit across all areas of our lives. We expect fast outcomes, and we are drafted into the cult of worshipping high expectations. From our jobs to our children to the things that we do in our spare time, we have unreasonable expectations and we expect them fast.

Excessive expectations are not characteristic of mental toughness. In fact, they work against it by creating pressures that stress the mind and can even push the mind to the breaking point. It's like trying to do body building with weights twice as heavy as you can lift. You might bulk up and get strong really quickly – or you could do permanent damage to your muscles. The latter is the more likely. Not a good bargain.

You invite patience in by casting aside expectations. By all means, set a goal, and strive toward it. Give yourself the room to make mistakes, and, when you do, learn from them. At the same time, keep pushing forward, keep working at it, but replace expectation with the faith that each step you take, whether success or failure, will ultimately lead you to the outcome you desire.

The way we usually look at expectations is all wrong. We think we should place high expectations on ourselves and others, as a way to motivate and push ourselves and others, but what we should have is faith – instead of expectations.

Having faith is what will allow you to have patience, and having patience contributes to mental toughness. Faith also adds a touch of grace to your life.

Patience is a way of controlling your own mind, a habit you can develop that will contribute to mental toughness. When you embrace patience, you begin to see that things get the chance to materialize for you, and that reduces the stress of expectations that can eventually erode mental toughness.

Faith is simply the certainty that something that you need will happen. In a sense, having faith automatically implies having patience. Faith doesn't need to be understood from a religious or spiritual perspective. Faith is an offshoot of a positive mindset and isn't "owned" by any particular religion. Faith is the vibration you operate under when you need something, and you are certain the universe will provide it. You can't do that without a positive mindset.

Conversely, if you have something, and you think you will lose it, that, too, will come to pass. So, you might as well have faith in good things happening. What do you have to lose?

A new look at a well-know and influential social science experiment from the 1960's and 1970's provides an interesting perspective on the relationship between patience and faith. In 1960, Walter Mischel conducted the famous "Marshmallow Test" with children at Stanford. The experiment measured the ability of a small group of children to delay gratification. Each child was videotaped as they were left alone in the room with one marshmallow for about 15 minutes, after being told by the tester that if they waited until the tester returned to take the marshmallow, they would be given a second one. Those children were followed years later to assess the correlation between their ability to wait and delay their gratification, and their life outcomes. This experiment found that the children who were able to wait longer had better life outcomes, a finding which has influenced numerous educators and social scientists since then.

However, more recent and better designed tests that have attempted to replicate the results and findings of the original "Marshmallow Test" have found something very different. These newer tests have suggested that it is the child's degree of belief that the tester will keep their promise that is determinant of both whether the child will eat the single marshmallow while the tester is absent and whether the child will have better life outcomes later.

So, what does this have to do with patience and faith? Everything.

The newer delayed-gratification tests of a child's ability to have patience are showing that it isn't the child's ability to exercise restraint through willpower and effort that matter, it's the child's faith that things will work out in the end. It is the confidence that a delayed outcome will be positive that matters – not only to the results of the immediate experiment, but also to long-term outcomes in all areas of life.

In other words, patience that is born of faith, that is, of an expectation that a delayed outcome will be positive, is more important than exerting willpower or effort to creating the kind of strength of mind that correlates with positive results throughout life.

Chapter 12: Endurance

The ability to endure through whatever may be going on in the moment is clearly related to qualities we have already looked at – a positive mindset and patience – that is, to the ability to expect a positive outcome, despite what may be going on in the moment. At its root, all endurance is mental, and it is a necessary quality for mental toughness. In fact, it is one of the qualities that most people think of when they consider someone as mentally tough.

The value of endurance is a little different from patience. Patience is about letting things bake, without hurrying it or getting frustrated while you wait. Endurance, on the other hand, is about actively doing something, repeatedly expending effort, despite negative or insufficient outcomes, until you achieve the outcome.

To be successful, you need to be able to fall and get back up again and again. It doesn't matter how many times you fall – it only matters when you decide to stop getting back up. As long as you keep trying, you are not a failure – you are just a work-in-progress.

This is another one of those reciprocal relationships, a road that goes in both directions.

If you never give up, you develop a stronger mind, and the stronger your mind gets, the less you will give up. One day you may even become like Edison or one of those diligent entrepreneurs who set their sights on accomplishing something and don't rest until they make it happen.

We tend to think of endurance as how much we can run, walk, or work, as a kind of marathon, as the distance we can go without running out of energy. In athletics, that can be an accurate description, but when it comes to our mental strength and the inner force that drives us, endurance is about how indifferent we are to the time it takes to achieve success at a task, or how much we need to do or go through to achieve our goal.

If you can envision a goal and commit to doing whatever it takes until that goal is attained, you will build your endurance. You can remind yourself to "do whatever it takes" in the moment, as a kind of a mental "hack." When you measure what you are doing against a distant goal, you can feel like you're stuck or standing still. Instead, if you don't benchmark the outcome to an arbitrary measure of time, you can put the importance on getting the objective completed, step by step, instead.

If you break your goals down into smaller bite-sized tasks, you can keep giving the mind the rewards it needs. The feeling of "success" is experienced as a reward. As a result, you will be more motivated to keep going. The mind focuses more easily on smaller tasks at hand than on those distant, overarching accomplishments with rewards in some far off future, those big goals that you have to relentlessly remind yourself to move toward.

Remember, you build mental endurance the same way you would build physical endurance – with practice. Endurance is practiced, not inherited. The more small objectives you set, the more you aspire to and successfully achieve, the more you will form a habit of enduring. It's like fasting. You start by skipping a meal. Then you skip two. Eventually, you can progress to skipping meals for a full day. In a short time, incrementally, you build up your endurance, and you can find yourself fasting for seven days in a row.

Whenever you want to build your endurance, whether it is in swimming, running, fasting, or succeeding, you need to take it up a notch at a time, using baby steps. There is no other way. One step at a time, without fail, without pause. Doing that, you will begin to experience the confidence that comes from having demonstrable evidence of being able to do what you once doubted or thought impossible. That confidence helps the mind endure even longer.

One of the best ways to develop mental toughness is to start with developing and practicing endurance. Weaker minds tend to give up, not because they don't know how to do something, but rather because they get tired and give up. Endurance has a lot to do with working through fatigue or discouragement.

That fatigue is much like the fatigue a marathon runner experiences. Fatigue is real and can be the difference between life and death. The willpower to go on in harsh conditions only goes so far. Sometimes, you need to keep going through the wall of fatigue. Other times, endurance is knowing when to take rest or a break in order to continue moving forward. Consider the soldier, of ancient legend, who ran from Marathon to Athens to tell the people that the battle had been won. He ran through the night, for 23 miles, without stopping once. He got to the town square, yelled "Nike," collapsed, and died of exhaustion.

There is something to be said for willpower. It can get you past the mistaken sensations of the body and the bouts of laziness we all have in these situations. But you should never push your mind and body so far that it breaks. There are times to heed the warning signs, and take care of your mind and body. That's one of the reasons to build up endurance gradually.

When you build physical endurance gradually, you give your body the time it needs to adjust. You need to do the same when you are building mental endurance. When you build it up slowly, your endurance will be more reliable and longer lasting.

One way to develop mental endurance is to set yourself mental challenges that require you to keep going in the face of frustration or other obstacles. You could, for instance, start doing crossword puzzles, forcing yourself to complete the entire thing. Each time, aim to reduce the time to complete the crossword by five percent. If it took you 60 minutes last time, aim for 57 minutes. Once you start, don't stop to do anything else, keep at it until it's done. If you pass the time allotted, don't stop, just keep going until you finish.

You can start playing a game that's a physical sport. Get your heart pumping while you are in a competitive state and go into the game with an intention to win – one point at a time. Play a full game through at least once a week.

Elite military persons, like Navy Seals or others, all go through rigorous training to develop endurance, to push past what they perceive to be their own limits, and to persist and ignore all the things that would pull them away from completing their task, no matter how onerous.

For more ordinary individuals, setting challenges like training for a marathon, or taking on some sort of 30-day challenge in a favorite subject, such as joining thousands of writers in their annual NaNoWriMo (National Novel Writing Month) challenge to write 50,000 words (a short book) during November, will build up endurance. You can build up your own endurance with activities like those, and, more importantly, train yourself to recognize that some of the limits you have been accepting as real have been self-imposed.

Chapter 13: Self-Control

It is nearly inconceivable to think of someone as having mental toughness without also having self-control. In fact, it's possible to argue that every topic covered in this book as an aspect of mental toughness is simply a different variety of self-control. Even perspectives, which we have said are at the heart of mental toughness, is also really about self-control, aren't they?

So, just what is self-control?

Self-control is an *executive function* of the brain. It's the cognitive process of self-regulating thoughts, actions, and emotions to achieve specific outcomes or goals. In psychology, it is considered an aspect of *inhibitory control*, that is, resisting temptations and impulses, rather than intentionally choosing thoughts, actions, and emotions.

However, for our purposes, we can simply define self-control as intentionally self-regulating and controlling what we think, act, and feel. Self-control can even extend into consciously controlling involuntary functions that aren't normally under conscious control, such as some functions of the autonomic nervous system.

At its simplest, self-control is just consciously deciding what you will think, do, and feel, rather than feeling, doing, and thinking automatically. That is harder to do than it may seem at first glance.

The average adult makes thousands of small and large decisions each and every day. The sheer number of decisions that a person makes can lead not only to overwhelm but also to decision fatigue. Becoming fatigued and overwhelmed works against self-control because it can lead to impulsive and irrational decisions. It also leads to falling back on default and automatic patterns.

Some of the same things that help with maintaining focus will also reduce being overwhelmed by too many decisions and will reduce decision fatigue. In particular, avoiding distractions and keeping input to a single stream will help both problems. When you can control distractions, you focus better, and you will make better decisions. However, there is more that you can do to specifically keep your self-control at its most effective.

For some time, the concept of *ego depletion* (a state of reduced willpower caused by a prior exercise of self-control) has been an accepted part of psychological and self-development literature. More recently, however, it has been called into question in the *replication crisis* sweeping those fields. Recent studies have not been able to demonstrate ego depletion.

Nevertheless, nearly anyone can validate a related idea from their own experience, and that is the idea of *decision fatigue* – a deterioration of the ability to make good decisions after a period of making a lot of decisions. Anyone who has had the experience of feeling that deciding "what's for supper" was too much after a particularly grueling day of making decisions will understand the impact that mental fatigue can have on self-control – as they default to the "easy" decision of dialing for pizza delivery.

Although the willpower to resist temptations and impulses isn't the whole story of what we are meaning by self-control, it is certainly part of what anyone interested in having better self-control wants. There are things that can specifically help with that:

1. Avoid temptations whenever possible – you don't have to exercise so much willpower when the thing you are trying not to do isn't right there.
2. Avoid fatigue and hunger, in general. Being tired or hungry will always make it harder to resist temptations and impulses.
3. Avoid being in environments where too many distractions and sensory inputs are coming at you all at once, because that will interfere with having the awareness and

focus to notice if you are about to do something that you are trying not to do.

4. Deal with the temptation of the moment, by taking it one day (or even one minute) at a time, rather than worrying about other times that you aren't yet dealing with.

5. Make sure to reinforce good choices by rewarding yourself, even if only with a pat on the back or feeling good about your choice.

Broadening out, though, to the idea of self-control as the making of conscious decisions on what to feel, think, and do, most of what you need to do is to establish the conditions that make genuine decision-making easier. That means you need to mitigate the effects of decision fatigue or avoid that fatigue altogether as much as possible.

One of the most important things you can do is to avoid overwhelming yourself with too many choices and decisions. It is very much like improving focus by limiting conscious inputs. Reduce how many choices and individual decisions you need to make through the course of a day. There are lots of ways to do that. Many of them will already be familiar – but what may be different is the idea of doing it for the sake of conscious self-control and decision-making.

When you look at successful people in any field or endeavor, you will find that they use many of these techniques to reduce the number of choices they have to make, so they can concentrate on important decisions – and you will see the result in the quality of the self-control they exhibit.

For example, it may seem like a small thing, but many uber-successful people have become known for wearing the same outfits every day. Here are just a few examples:

- Barack Obama – only wore black or grey suits during his presidency
- Mark Zuckerberg – grey t-shirt, blue jeans, and black hoodie
- Michael Kors – black suit, black t-shirt, black loafers, and black aviator glasses
- Simon Cowell – black or white t-shirt with jeans, or white shirt and jeans
- Steve Jobs – black mock turtleneck, jeans, and New Balance sneakers
- Giorgio Armani – cashmere sweaters and navy slacks
- Tom Wolfe – all white suit

Why? It eliminates the need to waste valuable mental resources first thing in the morning on deciding what to wear. Others, who would rather have more variety in their wardrobe, may lay out the next day's outfit the night before.

Whether the value of these practices comes from reducing the number of decisions or from reducing uncertainty for those who deal with high levels of uncertainty on a daily basis (and that is a debate), there is no doubt that they help conserve mental resources which are then more available for self-control.

Wearing the same thing every day falls under the umbrella of creating a routine of doing the same things in the same way, so the person doesn't need to "think" about it, eliminating those decisions. Other people have the same breakfast every day, or the same lunch. Some have the same bedtime routine. And, of course, many have workplace routines that they don't deviate from. Routines free up mental energy for other things, such as exercising greater levels of self-control.

Another old-fashioned strategy contributes to greater levels of self-control. Create good habits. Good habits are the thoughts, feelings, and actions you have decided (once) will move you in the direction you want to go. Do what you have already decided – over and over – and eventually it becomes automatic, a habit.

Better yet, the more good habits you have, the more they will displace those bad habits that tend to require great amounts of willpower to resist doing. Not only do you eliminate the need to use mental energy to decide (again and again) to do, think, or feel something desirable, you also stop wasting mental energy on resisting doing, thinking, or feeling something. Overall, this frees up loads of mental energy for self-control in other areas.

An entire category of things that makes having self-control easier comes down to planning or simplifying. For example, planning out the activities and priorities for the next day during the evening before reduces the number of decisions that need to be made throughout the day. Then you can tackle important things first, when you are fresh and focused.

In general, schedule things in ahead of time, blocking them off. That way, you don't need to "decide" to do them – you just need to go ahead and use your energy and resources to actually do what has already been decided.

Having self-control means that you can decide how you want to respond to any situation you encounter, decide how to feel, decide on the perspective you will take, decide to endure through stress. Self-control is sometimes misunderstood to mean self-discipline, but self-control really boils down to how you control yourself. The Romans had a saying – to rule the world you have to control yourself. Self-control is really about being "the boss of yourself."

As previously noted, self-control can be taken to extreme levels, even to controlling normally involuntary physiological functions. We tend not to realize just how much self-control of both our body and mind is available to us. For example, biofeedback training is an established modern method of helping people learn to self-control a broad range of problems, including anxiety, pain, high blood pressure, heart rate, muscle tension, and more. There are also many ancient techniques for self-control, such as various forms of yoga.

If you practice self-control at an advanced level, you may even be able to control things like headache pain without pills. I was forced to try that during my first 30-day fast. Everything was going well until I got a migraine on the fourth day. I often had them, but I hadn't planned how I would handle one during my fast. Instead of eating so I could take something for the pain, I decided to try focusing myself out of the pain. As I did breathing exercises and practiced focusing inward, the pain subsided within an hour. That was the first time I was able to control the pain of a migraine without pharmaceuticals.

With focus, you can learn to control pain. The sensations you feel are all in the brain. They are never in the location where you feel the pain. The nerve endings at the location of the injury send a signal to the brain, and the brain interprets that signal, lets your conscious mind know by giving you a sensation in that location, so that you'll know to attend to whatever is going on in that location. The pain, however, is not actually there. It is in your brain.

Pain and suffering are mental states we allow ourselves to endure. If you make the choice, you can release pain and suffering at almost every level. "Almost" because you don't want to rid yourself of pain entirely – you need pain to alert you to things that need to be attended to.

We tend to think of mentally tough people as being less affected by pain than others. That is the result of learning self-control. The mental toughness that comes with self-control can even keep you safe and alive. This is epitomized by Alexander the Great who was injured in the Siege of Male, when a spear, three inches in diameter, pierced his chest and bore a hole through his lung. He recovered and lived while others with smaller arrow wounds to legs and arms perished on the fields.

At one end of the spectrum, self-control is about choosing whether or not to eat an extra piece of cake for dessert. It's about whether you can will yourself to stop smoking or kick any habit. But as you progress toward the other end of the spectrum of self-control, you find that it starts to permeate into wider areas of your life. Ultimately self-control can include the ability to control pain and suffering.

Physical pain and intellectual suffering are born of the same strain, and they can both be vanquished by self-control. Entire religions have been built on the need to overcome pain and suffering, because it is one thing common to all human beings. Whether we live in view of the

117

Eiffel tower or under the shadow of the Himalayas, it is the part of the human condition to face one problem after another. We can accept suffering and become immune to it, or we can be mentally tough and transform that suffering into an opportunity. Self-control provides us with those options.

Having "book-ended" the subject of mental toughness on one end with "perspective" and "self-control" on the other, it could appear that we have come to the end of our discussion of mental toughness. Or have we? No. There is one more important element we haven't looked at yet.

Chapter 14: Acceptance

When all else fails, acceptance is the final bastion of mental toughness.

Who hasn't heard of the *Serenity Prayer*? This one prayer has given millions of people the momentary mental toughness to get through difficulties through the power of acceptance.

> *God, grant me the serenity to accept the things I cannot change,*
>
> *Courage to change the things I can,*
>
> *And wisdom to know the difference.*

Acceptance is the releasing of attachment to outcomes. Sometimes things do not work out the way one would want, and that is just the way of things. The poem's "serenity" is really the same peaceful non-attachment or detachment that allows one to pull back from negative experiences – and it is available to help endure through whatever *is*.

Acceptance is a recognized approach for dealing with difficult emotions and states of mind, far beyond the usual 12-step addiction recovery programs that have become associated with the *Serenity Prayer*. Acceptance is, in fact, a significant part of MBCT (Mindfulness-based Cognitive Therapy), therapeutic approaches for dealing with grief, and numerous spiritual and philosophical traditions.

Acceptance is a conscious process that needs to be actively practiced and can take effort. In its most basic sense, it means accepting what you cannot change in the present moment. Accepting "what is" or "reality" as it stands is the alternative to struggling against it. Resisting and rejecting what cannot be changed is the cause of much unnecessary suffering.

Accepting something doesn't mean that you want it, like it, approve it, or support it. It just means acknowledging what is and releasing the hope that it is different than it is. It doesn't necessarily mean forever – acceptance is in the present.

Acceptance is not about giving up, being passive, or being apathetic. And it is most definitely not abandoning personal agency. Acceptance is a conscious stance (perspective) that a person can choose and adopt toward anything that is outside of their own personal control. That includes accepting aspects of themselves that are outside of their control in the moment.

Sometimes the most mentally tough thing a person will ever have to do is to "accept" something, especially the "unacceptable." While acceptance demonstrates mental toughness, the practice of acceptance also builds mental toughness. It's another one of those reciprocal relationships.

Contentment with who you are and what you have right now is part of acceptance. Someone who is mentally tough isn't concerned with what the neighbor has, isn't resentful or envious. They accept who they are and what they have.

Contentment doesn't mean complacency. You can accept what you have, who you are, and where you are in any given moment, and still want things to be different or better. You can be content with your position and still be ambitious.

Mentally tough people are focused on the contribution they can make, knowing that the rewards can come later, not focused on the rewards that they can consume. Contribution brings success and its rewards, consumption creates lethargy. Contentment and acceptance of where you are, allows you to focus on your contribution rather than your consumption.

The opposites of acceptance are feelings like hatred, bitterness, and resentment. There is a Zen saying, that thinking ill of someone is like drinking poison and hoping the other person dies. In one of Will Smith's songs, he sings, "Hate in your heart will consume you too." You need to be careful what you think about. Mentally tough people understand that thinking ill of others, no matter how vile that person may be, really weakens themselves. Acceptance is the antidote to that poison.

Many spiritual traditions teach that the law of the universe is that you get more of whatever you focus on. If you focus on the bad things in life, you'll get a lot more of it. If you focus on your fears, you will end up having more fear and anxiety, or you will encounter the very things you fear. If you complain about what you don't have, you will get more of not-having.

By contrast, acceptance is the launching pad for more positive outcomes. Accepting where you are, even appreciating whatever positives it offers, goes hand-in-glove with "gratitude" which is taught as the way to bring more blessings toward yourself.

If you are dissatisfied with where you are and who you are, you are not practicing acceptance. You can want things to be better in the future and work toward that, while still accepting things as they are in the present moment.

With a final word from Viktor Frankl, we are brought full circle, "When we are no longer able to change a situation, we are challenged to change ourselves."

Conclusion

With that, we come to the end of the book but not to the end of the journey. If you pursue only one thing to improve yourself, mental toughness is the objective that will have the biggest impact on all areas of your life. Developing mental toughness benefits every part of your life. If you subscribe to the notion that you are what you think, then becoming mentally tough can make you into a new person.

In virtually every story of personal transformation that you have heard or will hear, the underlying theme is a change in perspective. Throughout this look at mental toughness, again and again, the notion of perspective has been invoked, whether explicitly or implicitly. That's not accidental. Every quality that contributes to mental toughness begins and ends with perspective. Taking charge of your perspective, in essence, is at the heart of every quality you need to have in order to be mentally tough.

* * *

If you have read this book in one go, as you probably just have, go back to the beginning and start to focus on one chapter at a time.

Grab a journal – and, as you approach each chapter for the second time, make notes of the thoughts that strike you and are relevant to your life. You will find that this kind of focused journaling can make a huge difference in your life and your self-awareness.

Becoming stronger and tougher mentally, in part, means shedding some of the things that hold you back – like Superman's kryptonite. As you read, you might recognize things that have been working as your own personal kryptonites. Make note of them – and of any ideas that come to you for counteracting, changing, or getting rid of those weaknesses.

Apply the exercises and ideas and write your experiences in your journal. Over time, you will be working your mind, like a muscle, making it more resilient, stronger, clearer. It will function more effectively, with more endurance. And, ultimately, you will find your mental toughness increasing, bit by bit.

* * *

May your personal journey to becoming more mentally tough transform you and your life in ways beyond what you can currently imagine.

If you enjoyed this book, I would be forever grateful if you could leave a review on Amazon. Reviews are the best way to help your fellow readers find the books worth reading so make sure to help them out! It would also help me out tremendously as reviews are the best validation a newer author can get. Thanks in advance!

rmation can be obtained
itesting.com
e USA
38180520
00003B/379